Dream Catchers

Activities

Third Edition

Career Development Projects

JIST Works

America's Career Publisher

Norene Lindsay

Dream Catchers Activities, *Third Edition*
Career Development Projects

© 2004 by JIST Publishing, Inc.

Published by JIST Works, an imprint of JIST Publishing, Inc.
8902 Otis Avenue
Indianapolis, IN 46216-1033

Phone: 800-648-JIST   Fax: 800-JIST-FAX
E-mail: info@jist.com   Web site: www.jist.com

> **Note to instructors.** *Dream Catchers Activities,* Third Edition, is part of a complete curriculum that includes a student workbook, a teacher's guide, and this book of reproducible activities. All materials are available separately from JIST.
>
> **Videos and other materials** on career exploration are also available from JIST. A CD-ROM and Web site with information on over 14,000 jobs is available through CareerOINK.com. The Web site offers information at free and subscription levels. Call 1-800-648-JIST for details.
>
> **Quantity discounts are available for JIST products.** Please call 1-800-648-JIST or visit www.jist.com for a free catalog and more information.
>
> **Visit www.jist.com.** Find out about our products, order a catalog, and link to other career-related sites. You can also learn more about JIST authors and JIST training available to professionals.

Acquisitions Editor: Randy Haubner
Development Editor: Veda Dickerson
Cover and Interior Designer: Aleata Howard
Interior Layout: Carolyn J. Newland
Proofreader: David Faust

Printed in the United States of America

07 06 05 04 03   9 8 7 6 5 4 3 2 1

ISBN 1-59357-003-1

About This Book

Schools across the nation are now emphasizing career development programs in the intermediate grades. This emphasis makes good sense because of the increasingly competitive global economy, the changing nature of work, and the importance of education and career planning to a student's success as an adult.

Specific guidelines for career awareness competencies at the intermediate level have been developed. These are known as the National Career Development Guidelines. The *Dream Catchers* curriculum fulfills many of the competencies related to self-knowledge, educational and occupational exploration, and career planning.

A great advantage of the *Dream Catchers* materials is that they can be integrated into any academic subject. They can also be used as a separate, complete career development curriculum. The reproducible activity sheets in this book are designed for easy integration into your classroom work. They allow you to expand and enhance career development concepts and strengthen academic skills.

There are three books in the *Dream Catchers* series. The *Dream Catchers* workbook is for your students. Supporting the workbook are two books to assist teachers using these materials in a classroom setting: *Dream Catchers Teacher's Guide* and *Dream Catchers Activities.* The curriculum can be used in an individual, small group, or classroom setting:

> *Dream Catchers:* This student workbook is designed to increase career awareness in the intermediate grades prior to high school. It includes interesting narrative and in-book activities.
>
> *Dream Catchers Teacher's Guide:* Provides interactive group or class lesson plans for each activity in the student workbook. Each lesson plan provides a learning objective or outcome in a step-by-step format for each activity.
>
> *Dream Catchers Activities:* This book provides more than 80 reproducible individual, small-group, or class activities to supplement the content of the student workbook.

(continues)

(continued)

To get the most out of these books, use them in conjunction with each other. This will minimize teacher preparation time and maximize student growth. The materials and related activities encourage thinking and interaction with others and some self-reflection. The many activities can be used sequentially to support a complete career awareness program. They can also be used to infuse career awareness into a variety of subjects.

Dream Catchers Activities follows the structure of the student workbook and then adds one additional part. Parts 1, 2, and 3 correspond to the same three parts in *Dream Catchers.* Part 4 of this guide provides activities and suggestions for creating your own unit on the relationship between work and the needs and functions of society.

Table of Contents

Part 2
The Stuff Dreams Are Made Of— Discovering Your Skills   52

Part 3
Making Dreams Come True—Ability, Effort, and Achievement   78

Part 4
Putting Your Dreams to Work—Work and the Needs and Functions of Society — 103

INDICES
Individual Activities

ACTIVITY SHEET
   NUMBER

©JIST Works

Small-Group Activities

ACTIVITY SHEET
NUMBER

Class Activities

ACTIVITY SHEET
NUMBER

Introduction

This book contains more than 80 reproducible activities that can be easily duplicated to supplement exercises in the student workbook, *Dream Catchers*. The activities are designed to enhance and expand the concepts explored in *Dream Catchers*. The *Dream Catchers Teacher's Guide* will give you complete instructions on how to integrate the activities easily into your lesson plans. While we believe that you will benefit from the helpful information found in the *Teacher's Guide*, it is not essential for using the reproducible activity sheets in this book.

Additional Photocopies

The activity sheets in this book are designed specifically for use with *Dream Catchers*. If you are using the book as a student text for classroom purposes, you are hereby authorized to make additional photocopies from this book as needed. Reproduction for other uses requires written approval from the publisher and typically requires a small fee.

Organization

The activities in this book are organized numerically to correspond to the three parts of the *Dream Catchers* book, as you will see in the Table of Contents. A fourth section on activities that relate to "Work and the Needs and Functions of Society" also is included, if you choose to pursue that topic.

Using the Activity Sheets

At the beginning of each activity sheet, you will find the Activity Sheet number and then an indication of how the activity can be used with your students. Following is a list of the three ways to use the activities:

- **Individual activity.** This designation indicates that the activity can be performed by the student alone. You can have the whole class do an individual activity at the same time, but they can also be done independently by some students.

- **Small-group activity.** This designation indicates that the activity can be performed in small groups. Some small-group activities require the use of small groups while others have the option of the student performing the activity independently.
- **Class activity.** This code designates that the activity requires participation by the whole class for at least part of the activity.

Indices

Indices organizing the activities by use (individual, small-group, or class) can be found in the Table of Contents. They allow you to quickly select the type of activity you want for your students. If an activity can be completed in more than one way, for example, by an individual or a small group, it is included in both indices.

Reproductions

Some of the activity sheets are reproductions of pages in *Dream Catchers.* These pages are reproduced because you may need to use them more than once. You might, for example, want your students to take home some of their goal-setting exercises to share with their parents, or if you have them research more than one career for instance, you will need to reproduce additional copies of the "Career Data Worksheet."

The *Teacher's Guide* indicates if a particular page in *Dream Catchers* is available as a reproducible activity sheet. The activity sheets also contain sheets representing each career cluster. These career cluster sheets are used in conjunction with other activities in this book.

Flexibility

The activities vary in the amount of time required for their completion. Some can be finished in as short a period as 15 minutes, and others require more time. A good mix of short, mid-range, and long-term projects are provided. You can use the activities in class or assign them as homework or extra-credit projects. Many of these activities require reading, language arts, social studies, math, and study skills. This simplifies integrating the activities into academic subjects if you choose.

Part 1

Capture Your Dreams—The Choice Is Yours

Write a Letter Home

Do the adults in your house ever ask you, "What did you do in school today?" Sometimes it's hard to answer! This activity will help you answer that question.

Directions

Write a letter home about your new *Dream Catchers* book. Your teacher will explain the correct letter form, or you can use your language book. If you mail the letter, address the envelope correctly.

- **Paragraph 1**—Give the title and the subtitle of your book. (Check your language book for the correct way to write book titles.) Explain that this is a new book you are starting to use.

- **Paragraph 2**—Copy the following information for your letter.

"Dream Catchers is a three-part book that will help me learn about the world of work. In Part 1, I will learn about different career choices and the skills needed to use career information. In Part 2, I will learn how schoolwork and jobs are connected. I will study the skills needed for both schoolwork and jobs. I also will learn about the different places to get education or training for jobs. In Part 3, I will learn how ability, effort, and achievement will help me be successful in school and when I get a job. This will give me lots of ways to improve my study skills and work habits."

- **Paragraph 3**—Explain that you will need help from your parent(s), guardian(s), or other adults when learning about work. You will interview them about the different kinds of work they do—jobs, volunteer work, or housework.

- **Paragraph 4 (optional)**—You could explain the Indian legend about dream catchers, which on the "What Is a Dream Catcher?" page in your *Dream Catchers* book. You even could draw a dream catcher on the back of your letter.

Extra Activity

Letter Exchange

Exchange letters with a classmate. Proofread one another's letter. Make sure they are written in the correct form. Check for punctuation and spelling errors. Write a final, corrected copy of your letter.

4

Make Your Own Dream Catcher

Directions

Follow the steps below to make a dream catcher. (Look at the cover of this book for help.) You can add other decorations if you wish—this is your own creation!

Step 1: Making the Frame

1. Cut one piece of waxed string about 6 inches long.

2. Take one long grapevine (16 to 20 inches) and make a mark in the middle of it.

3. Shape half the grapevine into a circle. Take one end and bend it to the middle mark.

4. Twist the straight half of the grapevine around the circle you just made by going over and under the circle.

5. Tie the grapevine ends together with waxed string where they meet. You can tie any "loose spots" on the frame with waxed string too.

Materials Needed

■ Bendable materials to make the dream catcher frame. You can use grapevines or any branches or twigs that are soft enough to bend into a circle without cracking. Note: Many craft or garden stores sell grapevine wreaths that can be taken apart to make several frames.

■ Waxed string. (Available in craft or leather stores.)

■ A large feather at least 6 inches long. (Use a real one or make one from construction paper and pipe cleaners.)

■ Beads or other decorations. (One bead should have a center hole about 3/8 inch in diameter.)

Step 2: Making the Web

1. Measure the width of your frame. Cut six pieces of waxed string that are at least 6 inches longer than the frame's width.

2. Take one piece of string and tie it to the frame. Tie the other end on the opposite side. Tie the string tight.

3. Take another piece of string. Repeat the step above. Tie this string across the frame so the circle is divided into four equal sections.

4. Make two marks on the frame in each of the four sections. This divides each section into thirds. (You make a total of eight marks on your frame.)

5. Tie a piece of string to a mark in one section. Tie the end of the same string to the mark on the exact opposite side of the frame. Repeat this step with the three strings left. When you finish, your frame consists of 12 sections.

6. Cut a piece of string about 15 inches long. Tightly tie that string to any string on your frame, about ¾-inch away from the frame.

7. Take the string and weave it in a circle around all the strings. To weave, pass the string under the frame string. Bring it up and around the frame string again to form a "loop." Pull the loop so it is tight. Make another "loop" on the next string tied to the frame. Repeat this step until you have made a complete circle. Tie a knot when you finish the circle. Cut off any extra string.

8. Make as many "inner circles" as you want to finish your web.

Step 3: Adding the Feather

1. Take the feather and slip a bead with a 3/8-inch hole on the "quill" end of it. Push the bead about 2 inches from the end of the feather. (If you make your own feather, use a pipe cleaner for the quill end.)

2. Put the feather in the center of your dream catcher web where all the strings cross. Bend the quill so it is on the other side of the crossed strings.

3. Push the bead up so it covers the bent quill end. This will hold your feather to the web.

Step 4: Finishing Your Dream Catcher

1. Tie a strong loop to the top of your dream catcher for hanging.

2. Cut off any extra string hanging from your dream catcher frame, or you can tie beads on the string ends for decoration.

Make Your Own Cluster Games

In *Dream Catchers*, you learned about clusters. A *cluster* is a group of things that are put together because they are alike in some ways. This activity shows you how to make three cluster games. You can have fun with clusters! Other ideas for games are on the back of this sheet.

Directions

Follow the steps below to play each of the cluster games.

Name That Cluster!

1. Make two columns on a sheet of paper. Label the left-hand column, "Things in the Cluster." Label the right-hand column, "Cluster Name."

2. List the names of things that can be grouped together under the "Things in the Cluster" column. (Try to think of several different groups.) Leave the "Cluster Name" column blank. For example:

THINGS IN THE CLUSTER

					CLUSTER NAME
1. Apple	Orange	Banana	Grape	Pear	

3. Give your paper to a classmate. Try to guess the cluster names.

Cluster Cards

1. Write four different cluster names on a sheet of paper. List five things that would fit into each cluster. Don't let anyone see your paper.

2. Make 20 cards using notebook paper or index cards.

   Fold the long sides of notebook paper in half. Then fold the paper in half from top to bottom. You will have four rectangles. Tear along the fold lines to make your cards. Repeat the process until you have 20 cards.

3. Write one name of one thing in your clusters on each card. When you are done, each card will have a different name on it.

4. Mix up all your cards. Give them to a classmate. Have your classmate arrange the cards into four clusters. Then she or he can try to guess the name of each cluster.

More Cluster Games

Clusters can be made from many things. You even can use cluster games to help study and review your schoolwork! You can make clusters from the subjects you are studying now. Use your textbooks to help. Some examples are given below:

- **Language**—Make clusters of nouns, verbs, adjectives, adverbs, book titles, or quotations.

- **Math**—Number clusters can be great fun. They can be real "brainteasers" when trying to guess the cluster name. For instance, you might group numbers that can be divided by 6, numbers that end in 2, even numbers, or fractions. Try to stump your classmates.

- **Spelling**—Make clusters of words that have silent *e*'s, double vowels, or compound words.

- **Social Studies**—Make clusters of mountain ranges, countries in Europe, names of lakes, or state capitals.

- **Science**—Make clusters of flowering plants, mammals, types of weather, or natural resources.

Career Cluster Collages

A *collage* is a way to make a piece of art. You lay out different materials and paste them on a hard surface.

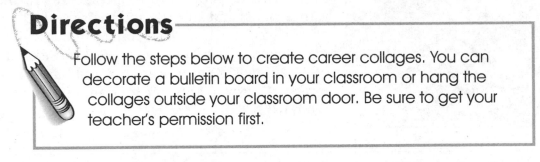

Directions

Follow the steps below to create career collages. You can decorate a bulletin board in your classroom or hang the collages outside your classroom door. Be sure to get your teacher's permission first.

1. Divide the class into nine small groups. Each group will be assigned a different career cluster.

2. Each group should get a "Career Cluster Worksheet" from your teacher.

3. As a group, think of lots of jobs that belong in your cluster. Write the job names on the "Career Cluster Worksheet." You can use the jobs listed in your *Dream Catchers* book to get started.

4. Each group member should look through magazines and newspapers at home to find pictures of people working at jobs in your cluster. You also can draw or trace pictures.

5. Get a poster board or a piece of cardboard.

6. Lay out your collage. Trim your pictures into different shapes. When making a collage, many pictures overlap. You don't want any poster board to show. Place your "Career Cluster Worksheet" and your pictures on your poster board. Experiment with different layouts.

7. Paste your "Career Cluster Worksheet" and pictures to your poster board.

Plants and Animals Cluster Worksheet

In this cluster, people breed, grow, care for, and gather plants and animals and their products. They also catch, hunt, and trap animal life. They may do work like: 1) grow crops; 2) raise cattle or other animals; 3) grow, care for, and harvest forests; 4) grow plants in a greenhouse; or 5) catch fish.

_____

_____

_____

_____

_____

_____

_____

_____

_____

_____

_____

_____

_____

_____

_____

_____

_____

Business and Marketing Cluster Worksheet

In this cluster, people have jobs that keep businesses running every day. They may do work like: 1) make plans; 2) give directions to other people; 3) sell things; 4) talk to customers; 5) do letters and reports; 6) work on a computer or other business machines; or 7) keep track of money.

_____

_____

_____

_____

_____

_____

_____

_____

_____

_____

_____

_____

_____

_____

_____

_____

Arts, Entertainment, and Media Cluster Worksheet

In this cluster, people create things to express ideas, thoughts, or feelings. They may do work like: 1) draw pictures by hand or on a computer; 2) write stories or newspaper articles; 3) take photographs; 4) act in a play or movie; 5) play music or sing; 6) arrange flowers; or 7) talk on TV or radio.

_____

_____

_____

_____

_____

_____

_____

_____

_____

_____

_____

_____

_____

_____

Construction and Production Cluster Worksheet

In this cluster, people build, fix, and make things. *Construction workers* may do work like: 1) build a house, building, bridge, or road; 2) put in plumbing; 3) fix a road; or 4) operate a bulldozer. *Production workers* may do work like: 1) put together a car; 2) take coal out of mines; 3) make tools; and 4) build furniture.

_____

_____

_____

_____

_____

_____

_____

_____

_____

_____

_____

_____

_____

Education, Human Services, and Personal Service Cluster Worksheet

In this cluster, people teach or help other people. *Education workers* may do work like: 1) teach children or adults; or 2) help people find books in a library. *Human services workers* may do work like: 1) listen to people's problems and try to help solve them; and 2) help people understand the law. *Personal service workers* may do work like: 1) cut or style hair; 2) take care of lawns; 3) prepare food; 4) guard or protect people or things; or 5) fight fires.

_____

_____

_____

_____

_____

_____

_____

_____

_____

_____

_____

Health Cluster Worksheet

In this cluster, people try to prevent illness. They also take care of people or animals who are sick. They may do work like: 1) take care of sick people in a hospital or at home; 2) give shots; 3) make medicine; 4) fix teeth; 5) run tests in a lab; 6) take X rays; or 7) give eye and hearing tests.

_____

_____

_____

_____

_____

_____

_____

_____

_____

_____

_____

_____

_____

_____

_____

Repairers, Installers, and Mechanics Cluster Worksheet

In this cluster, people fix and take care of all kinds of big and small machines. They may do work like: 1) repair dents in cars and trucks; 2) check airplane engines; 3) fix broken TVs or VCRs; 4) repair robots or computers; 5) erect electric power lines; 6) fix machines in a factory; or 7) repair watches.

Science and Technology Cluster Worksheet

In this cluster, people do scientific research to discover, collect, and analyze knowledge. They use this knowledge to solve problems or invent new things. They may do work like: 1) try to find a cure for a disease; 2) test food for safety; 3) improve airplane designs; 4) discover ways to stop pollution; 5) invent new products or things; or 6) predict earthquakes.

_____

_____

_____

_____

_____

_____

_____

_____

_____

_____

_____

_____

_____

Transportation Cluster Worksheet

In this cluster, people help move people or things from one place to another. They may do work like: 1) drive a taxi, bus, truck, or train; 2) fly an airplane; 3) help passengers on an airplane, ship, or train; 4) guide planes from the ground; 5) move boxes and large objects; or 6) load or take things off a ship.

_____

_____

_____

_____

_____

_____

_____

_____

_____

_____

_____

_____

You Work with People and Animals Too!

In *Dream Catchers,* you learned that jobs can be put into different groups. Jobs can be grouped by who or what people do most of their work with. One of these groups was "People and Animals."

In this group, people spend most of their time working with other people or animals. Their jobs involve helping or serving people or animals. For example, a nurse, a teacher, a taxi driver, a salesperson, a zookeeper, and a veterinarian all work with people or animals.

Directions

Think of all the activities you do with other people or animals. Write them on the lines below.

_____

_____

_____

_____

_____

_____

_____

_____

_____

_____

_____

_____

©JIST Works

Extra Activity

Make a Class List of People and Animal Activities

1. Work in a small group. Collect everyone's worksheet on people and animal activities. Divide the worksheets among group members.

2. Read aloud the worksheet with the longest list. Have group members cross out an activity if it's on their worksheet. Compare what's left on all worksheets. Cross out duplicates.

3. Get a marker and a big sheet of paper. Next write "People and Animal Activities" on the top. Write your group's list on the paper. Hang your list in the classroom.

You Work with Things and Machinery Too!

In *Dream Catchers*, you learned that jobs can be put into different groups. Jobs can be grouped by who or what people do most of their work with. One of these groups was "Things and Machinery."

In this group, people work every day with things or machinery. They work with things that are not alive. For example, a carpenter, a factory worker, an automobile repair person, a laboratory scientist, and a computer operator work with things or machinery.

 **Directions**

Think of all of the activities you do with things and machinery. Write them on the lines below.

_____

_____

_____

_____

_____

_____

_____

_____

Extra Activity

Make a Class List of Things and Machinery Activities

1. Work in a small group. Collect everyone's worksheet on things and machinery activities. Divide the worksheets among group members.

2. Read aloud the worksheet with the longest list. Have group members cross out an activity if it's on their worksheet. Compare what's left on all worksheets. Cross out duplicates.

3. Get a marker and a big sheet of paper. Write "Things and Machinery Activities" on the top. Next, write your group's list on the paper. Hang your list in the classroom.

You Work with Data Too!

In *Dream Catchers,* you learned that jobs can be put into different groups. Jobs can be grouped by who or what people do most of their work with. One of these groups was "Data."

In this group, people work every day with information and facts. They may explain, collect, organize, or study information. For example, a newspaper editor, a police artist, a chemist, a weather person, and a safety inspector all work with information and facts.

Some people gather information and facts and use them in new or creative ways. This activity is described as having ideas. For example, a writer, an artist, an inventor, and a designer all use data in creative or new ways.

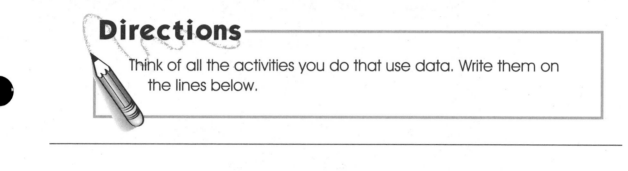

Directions

Think of all the activities you do that use data. Write them on the lines below.

_____

_____

_____

_____

_____

_____

_____

_____

_____

_____

_____

Extra Activity

Make a Class List of Data Activities

1. Work in a small group. Collect everyone's worksheet on data activities. Divide the worksheets among group members.

2. Read aloud the worksheet with the longest list. Have group members cross out an activity if it's on their worksheet. Compare what's left on all worksheets. Cross out duplicates.

3. Get a marker and a big sheet of paper. Write "Data Activities" on the top. Next, write your group's list on the paper. Hang your list in the classroom.

Discovering More Working Conditions

In *Dream Catchers,* you learned that jobs could be grouped by their working conditions. You did an activity on the working conditions "Inside" and "Outside." But there are more working conditions.

Directions

Other kinds of working conditions are described here. Make lists of jobs with that working condition on the lines provided. (Give a job title or describe the job.)

Both Inside and Out

Workers spend about half their time inside buildings or in something that protects them from weather. They also spend half their time outside.

_____

_____

_____

_____

Noise Level

Workers are exposed to really high noise levels. The noise can bother workers or cause hearing loss.

_____

_____

_____

_____

Temperature

Workers do work in really hot or cold temperatures. Their bodies will react to the temperatures—hot or cold.

_____

_____

_____

_____

Safety

Workers do work under conditions that can cause danger to life and health or cause risk of getting injured.

_____

_____

_____

_____

Extra Activity

You can do this activity in small groups. Compete with one another. The group with the most jobs for all categories wins.

Conduct a Workforce Survey

In *Dream Catchers,* you learned that workers can be employees or self-employed. *Employees* are workers who work for others. *Self-employed* means that you work for yourself.

Most people work as employees. Yet the number of self-employed people is growing every year. As a class, do a workforce survey. Discover how many people you know who are employees or self-employed. (In a *survey* you gather data and analyze the results.)

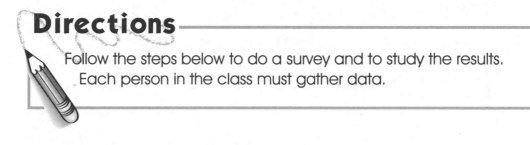

Directions

Follow the steps below to do a survey and to study the results. Each person in the class must gather data.

1. Ask at least five adults if they are employees or self-employed. (Record the answers on the back of this paper.) Also ask them for their job titles.

2. Bring your research to class.

3. Add the total number of employees and the total number of self-employed people from all data gathered.

4. Figure out the percentage of employees and self-employed people from your survey. (Your teacher can help you with this step.)

5. Make a list of the jobs self-employed people work at from your data. Do they do the same kind of work as employees? How many different kinds of self-employed jobs did you find?

Learning About Self-Employment

In *Dream Catchers*, you learned that some people choose to work for themselves. They are called self-employed. Because of technological advances like computers and fax machines, many more opportunities exist for people to be self-employed. Many self-employed people even work out of their homes. The number of self-employed people in the workforce is growing. Self-employment may be a real career option for you. To learn how self-employment is different from being an employee, find someone you know who is self-employed and interview her or him.

Directions

Interview a self-employed person. Some questions to ask are listed below, but you can ask other questions too. Write a report from your interview to share with your class.

- What kind of work do you do?

- Where do you work?

- How did you decide to work for yourself?

- Did you work for someone else before you started your own business? What did you do?

- Do you work alone or do you have employees?

- What do you like about being self-employed?

- What do you dislike about being self-employed?

- If I wanted to have my own business some day, what advice can you give me?

Activity Sheet #20
Individual activity

Career Data Worksheet

My name: _____

Date: _____

Source(s) of information: _____

Job title: _____

_____

In what career cluster does this job belong?

_____

Is the work mostly with data, people and animals, or things and machinery?

_____

What are the working conditions? Describe the workplace. _____

_____

_____

_____

If you did this work, would you probably be an employee or self-employed?

_____

Describe the kind of work done on this job. _____

_____

_____

_____

©JIST Works

Describe the skills needed for this job. _____

_____

_____

_____

_____

Where can the skills for this job be learned? _____

_____

_____

_____

_____

Can either a man or woman do this job? (Yes or No) Explain why. _____

_____

_____

_____

_____

_____

_____

Write a Letter to Ask for Career Information

Many places offer free brochures that give information on specific jobs. Write a letter of inquiry (*inquiry* means to ask for something) for information on a career that you like. Your teacher can help you find the addresses of places to write. Follow the instructions below.

Directions

A letter of inquiry has six parts: heading, inside address, greeting, body, closing, and signature. Write your letter following the steps below.

1. **Heading**—Write your address and the date on the top right-hand side of your paper. Skip two lines.

2. **Inside Address**—Write "Career Information Director" and the address you are writing to at the left-hand margin. Skip a line.

3. **Greeting**—Write "Dear Career Information Director:"

4. **Body**

   - **Introduction**—Give your name, grade, and school. Tell the person you are studying about careers in your class.

   - **Body**—Write a paragraph asking for any free brochures or information on the career you select. Make sure to name the career. Tell the person why you want the information.

   - **Closing**—Write a paragraph thanking the person for sending you the information. Tell him or her you are looking forward to getting it.

5. **Closing**—Write "Sincerely yours,"

6. **Signature**—Write your first and last name.

7. **Envelope**—Write your full name and address (including the ZIP code) in the upper left-hand corner. Address the envelope to "Career Information Director" and use the full inside address in the letter. Check your language book for examples if needed.

Careers of Famous People

A *biography* or *autobiography* is the story of a person's life. Sometimes people are famous because of their work. Read a biography or autobiography that describes someone's life and work. Your librarian can help you find a book.

Directions

Read the biography or autobiography. Write a book report answering the questions below. Skip any questions that your book doesn't answer.

1. What is the book title; who is the author; and how many pages does the book contain?

2. What kind of work did this person do that made him or her famous? Describe some of this person's accomplishments.

3. How did the person get interested in this kind of work?

4. Did the person have any special training or education to learn the work? How did she or he learn the skills needed for the job?

5. Did the person have to try very hard to accomplish his or her goals? What did she or he do? How long did it take?

6. Did this person have any failures before he or she succeeded? What happened?

7. What part of this book did you like the most? Why?

8. Would you like to do this kind of work? Explain why or why not.

Make a Career Cluster Handbook

When the class finishes its career research using "Career Data Worksheets," make a handbook with all the worksheets. Keep this book in your classroom library for studying.

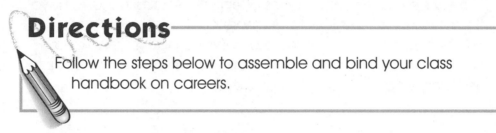

Directions

Follow the steps below to assemble and bind your class handbook on careers.

1. Divide the worksheets into career cluster groups. Each separate cluster will be a chapter in your book.

2. Divide the class into small groups. Assign each group one cluster to work with.

3. Get another "Career Cluster Worksheet" that matches your cluster from your teacher.

4. Alphabetize the "Career Data Worksheets" in your cluster by the job title.

5. List the job titles in your cluster on the "Career Cluster Worksheet" in alphabetical order. This activity sheet will be the Table of Contents for your cluster.

6. Proofread to correct any errors in your "Career Data Worksheets." (You may need to copy some of the worksheets again.)

> **Optional:** *You may want to draw illustrations for the jobs in your cluster or bring in pictures from magazines. If you use magazine pictures, paste them on a piece of notebook paper.*

7. Organize your chapter. Put the "Career Cluster Worksheet" first, and then the "Career Data Worksheets" in alphabetical order.

8. Select someone or a group to draw a cover for the handbook on an 8½-x-11-inch sheet of paper. Insert or paste the cover on a 3-ring binder notebook.

9. Three-hole punch all the pages and put them in the notebook in the correct alphabetical order.

10. Select someone to make a Table of Contents for the whole handbook that lists all the clusters in alphabetical order.

Extra Activity

Career Cluster Research

If you have clusters with no jobs or only a few jobs in them, have class members volunteer to do more career research in that cluster. If you learn about more careers during the year, add them to the class handbook. You can donate your handbook to the library when the school year is over.

Plan a Job Fair

A *job fair* is when different workers gather together to explain their job to an audience. You've already researched jobs using your "Career Data Worksheet." Now you can explain this work to an audience.

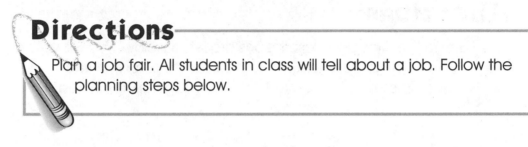

Directions

Plan a job fair. All students in class will tell about a job. Follow the planning steps below.

1. Select a career you want to present from your "Career Data Worksheets."

2. Use the worksheet to decide what you will tell the audience. (Know the information so well you don't have to read it.)

3. Select a day for your job fair. (Your teacher will help.)

4. On the day you present your job, bring to class any special tools your job choice may require.

5. Dress the part! Wear the clothes a person would normally wear for that job.

6. Ask for questions from the audience when you have finished your presentation.

Extra Activity

Share Your Information

Your class might like to invite another class to attend your job fair.

Write a Wild Work Story!

Did you know that in the United States over 12,000 different job titles exist? That's a lot of jobs! This activity involves jobs that you probably have never heard about.

Directions

Some job titles and descriptions are listed below. You will write a story using those jobs. Try to include lots of jobs in your story. The more the better! Let your imagination run wild!

1. **Custom Bow Maker**—selects, laminates, shapes and finishes wood, plastic, and metal to make archery bows.

2. **Makeup Artist**—applies makeup to performers to change their appearances to fit the parts they are playing.

3. **Seismologist**—studies and interprets information to find earthquakes and earthquake faults.

4. **Siviculturist**—plants new trees and takes care of forests to make sure the trees grow well.

5. **Horse Exerciser**—rides racehorses to exercise and condition them for horse racing.

6. **Airline Security Representative**—checks passengers for weapons, explosives, or other forbidden items. Prevents people from taking them into the airport or on an airplane.

7. **Rocket Engine Component Mechanic**—puts together and tests the mechanical parts of rocket engines.

8. **Chef de Froid**—designs and prepares decorated foods. Artistically arranges foods for buffets in fancy restaurants.

9. **Laser-Beam Machine Operator**—operates a laser-beam machine, which produces heat from a light beam to weld metal parts together.

10. **Telecommunicator**—operates communication equipment. Sends people and equipment to the scene of an emergency.

11. **Cryptographic Machine Operator**—operates cryptographic machines to code, send, and decode secret messages for the military, police departments, or businesses.

Pick Your "Dream" Career

It's always fun to dream, so let's do it. If you could pick a career for one day, what would you choose? A movie star? A professional sports figure? President of the United States? A rock singer? An astronaut? A surgeon? For this activity, you can pick any job you like.

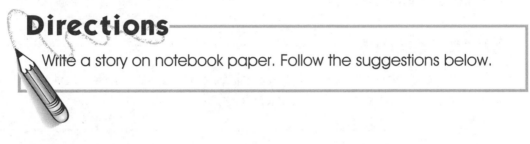

Directions

Write a story on notebook paper. Follow the suggestions below.

1. **Title**

   Give your story this title:

   One Day in the Life of a _____ (fill in your job title).

2. **First paragraph**

   Tell the reader what your job is and give a short definition of it.

3. **Next paragraph**

   Write two to three paragraphs explaining your activities during a typical day at your job.

What's My Line?

There once was a quiz show on television called, *What's My Line?* A guest would come on the show, and then a group of four people, called the *panel*, would ask the guest questions. The panel had to try to guess the guest's job. The panel had to ask questions that could be answered "Yes" or "No." They had to guess the job in 20 questions or the guest won.

Directions

Your class can have a lot of fun playing *What's My Line?* Follow these directions to get ready to play.

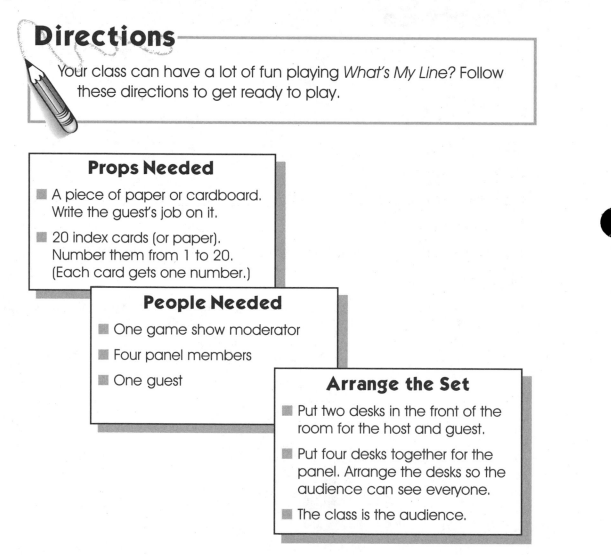

Props Needed

- A piece of paper or cardboard. Write the guest's job on it.

- 20 index cards (or paper). Number them from 1 to 20. (Each card gets one number.)

People Needed

- One game show moderator

- Four panel members

- One guest

Arrange the Set

- Put two desks in the front of the room for the host and guest.

- Put four desks together for the panel. Arrange the desks so the audience can see everyone.

- The class is the audience.

Game Rules

1. The moderator brings out the panel and introduces panel members to the audience.

2. The moderator then brings out the guest and introduces him or her.

3. The moderator shows the audience the card with the guest's job on it. Don't let the panel see! (On the TV show, the panel wore blindfolds for the whole game! You can do that too.)

4. The panel asks questions to try to guess the job. The questions can be answered only "Yes" or "No." If they ask a question that can't be answered "Yes" or "No," the moderator will say it's an illegal question. The panel member must change the question. Panel members take turns asking questions until 20 questions have been asked.

5. The moderator has the 20 numbered cards with number 20 on the top. The audience and panel must be able to see them. Each time a question is asked, the moderator removes one card. Then everyone knows how many questions are left.

6. After 20 questions have been asked, each panel member has one chance to guess the job. For example, "Are you a fireman?" If no one guesses correctly, the guest wins the game. (Or you can let the audience guess. See the "Optional Rule" below.)

> **Optional Rule:** *Do not show the guest's job to the audience. The panel might not guess the job after 20 questions. Then the moderator may call on people in the audience. They can try to guess the job.*

Hints for Playing

- **Ask good questions.** Use your new knowledge about careers to try to guess the job. You can ask the guest if he or she works with People and Animals, Things and Machinery, or Data. You can ask about the career cluster or the working conditions. Does the job require special education or training?

- **Make sure the guest knows the job.** People playing guests need many facts about the job. They should pick a job they have researched. The guest can use a "Career Data Worksheet" to answer questions. A guest also can ask the teacher for help in answering questions.

Work in Early America

In social studies, you learned how Americans lived in the past. Think of the time when America was a new nation. People lived very differently in those times than we do now.

When times change, the work people do also changes. For example, one job that no longer exists is wagon making. The way work is done also changes. For example, most women used to sew by hand all the clothes for their family. Now clothes are made on sewing machines, often in factories. People buy their clothes in stores. This activity will show you how work is different now.

Directions

Use your social studies book and library books to learn about America's early settlers. Everyone might read a book about America's early days. Then follow the steps below. You can do this activity alone or in small groups.

1. Write the titles below on separate sheets of paper.

    - Early American Jobs That Are Now Gone

    - Early American Work Done by One or Few People Now Done by Businesses or in Factories

    - Things We Buy That the Early Settlers Made for Themselves

    - Household Work and Chores Early Settlers Did That No Longer Exist

2. Make lists under each title using markers. Try to make long lists. Add drawings if you want. Display the lists in the classroom.

Props Needed

- 4 large sheets of paper
- Magic markers

Inventions Create Jobs!

When something new is invented, the invention can create new jobs. You might need people to make it, use it, repair it, or sell it. Just think of all the jobs created by Thomas Edison's inventions with electricity. This activity will show you how new jobs are created.

 **Directions**

Use your social studies book to research early inventions. Some examples are the telegraph, light bulb, and steam engine. Learn about more recent inventions like the telephone, television, VCR, computer, and airplane. Then follow the steps below.

1. Make a list of the inventions that have changed the way people live.

2. Pick one invention from the list you made in #1. Think about the new jobs created from that invention. Now make another list about those jobs. Give the list a title, for example, "Jobs Created by the Invention of the Telephone." Under that title, list all of the new jobs.

3. You may do this activity in small groups. As a class, make a list of inventions. Then divide the list among several small groups. Have each group make lists of jobs created by the inventions.

Jobs of the Future

You know that inventions create new jobs. People always are inventing new things. That means new jobs keep being created! What kind of jobs will exist in the future? This activity will help you guess.

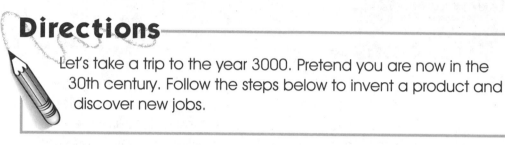

Directions

Let's take a trip to the year 3000. Pretend you are now in the 30th century. Follow the steps below to invent a product and discover new jobs.

1. "Invent" a product people can buy in the future. For example, your product could be a "Personal Robot."

2. Give your product a name. Write a description of what it looks like and what it does. It could be something people use, wear, or eat. You can even draw a picture of it.

3. Make a list of jobs now needed because of your invention. Give the list a title, for example, "Jobs Created by the Invention of the Personal Robot."

Optional: *Give your invention description to someone else. Have that person make a list of jobs now because of your invention.*

Job Genealogy

Genealogy is the study of ancestry or family histories. (We often call this "building a family tree.") To see how jobs change, study the kinds of jobs people in a family have had.

Directions

To build a job family tree, first select a family to research. You can use your own family, a relative's family, or a neighbor's family. You will do your research using interviews.

1. Decide which side of the family you will research. (You can research both sides of the family—mother and father—or only one side.)

2. Go back as far in the family history as the people being interviewed can remember (for example, great-grandparents or great-great-grandparents).

3. Ask the following questions. (Start with the oldest family member the person you are interviewing can remember. Work down to your generation.)

   • Name of the family member.

   • Name of the job(s) the family member has had. (Many people work more than one job in a lifetime. Make sure to include all the jobs that person had as an adult. Also, make sure to include homemaking as a job. If they can't remember certain people's jobs, put "unknown" on the family tree.

4. Your teacher will show you how to draw a genealogical chart (family tree). Draw a genealogical chart using the data you gathered in your research.

Workplaces in Your Community

Many workplaces in your community need different kinds or workers to operate the business. Think about all the places you've been where people work: a supermarket, department store, hospital, library, restaurant, or gas station. Do people in those workplaces have different jobs?

Directions

This activity will help you explore workplaces in your community and the different jobs people do in the same workplace. Follow the steps below to learn more about where people work.

1. Choose a workplace in your community. Draw a big picture of it.

2. Describe all the different kinds of jobs people do in that workplace. For example, a grocery store has cashiers, baggers, stockers, and many other jobs. Write the jobs on a piece of paper.

3. Attach your job descriptions to your picture.

4. Display your picture in your classroom. Your class could do a "Workplaces in Our Community" bulletin board.

Volunteer Work in Your Community

In *Dream Catchers,* you learned that many people work for free. This is called *volunteer* work. Find someone who has done volunteer work. Interview the person to learn what she or he did.

Directions

Sample interview questions are listed below. You can add any other questions you want. Write the person's name and the answers on notebook paper.

1. What volunteer work have you done? Describe as many volunteer activities as possible.

2. How did you find out about doing volunteer work?

3. Did you need any special training to do your volunteer work? If so, how did you get the training?

4. Why do you do volunteer work?

5. Do you think everyone should do volunteer work? Why?

Extra Activity

Report on Volunteer Work

1. Share your research with your classmates. Write a report about volunteer work from your interview. You might read your report out loud. Also, your teacher may have the class do a "volunteer work" bulletin board.

2. Compare everyone's research results. Make a big list of all the different kinds of volunteer work the class learned about. Hang your list in the classroom.

Plan a Class Volunteer Project

People often do volunteer work. Sometimes they help others. They might also work to improve the environment where they live. As a class, plan a volunteer project. You can help others or improve the environment.

You can select a simple project. Cleaning your school yard might be good. Helping students in lower grades could be fun. You also can select a more complex project. You could earn money and donate it to a charity. Or you could buy something your school needs. The instructions below are for a complex project that takes more time and planning. If you select a simple project, your teacher can help you plan it.

Directions

Decide what your class money-making project will be. You can have a garage sale. The class can bring in toys, books, and other items to sell. You may decide to make something to sell like popcorn and lemonade. Or you might decide to bake something simple to sell during lunch. Decide how you will use the money you earn.

Planning Your Project

Decide what tasks you must do. This list below gives suggestions. Make a list of tasks for your project.

- How will you gather the items to sell for a garage sale?

- If you make something to eat or drink, how much should you make? (For example, how many bags of popcorn will you need?)

- What ingredients will you need to make your product? Will you need to package your product? (For example, if you sell popcorn, will you put it in bags? Do you need to buy cups for drinks?)

- If you need to buy supplies, how much will you buy? How much will it cost? (These costs are your expenses.) Who will buy the supplies you need? Where will you get the money? (You may need to take out a business loan.)

- Will you have other expenses? For example, if you bake something, how much will the ingredient cost?

- Figure out your estimated profit. Subtract your expenses from how much money you think you will make.

- How will you advertise your project? How often? Do you need to make a handout for classmates to take home?

- Do you need to get permission from your principal? Should you ask other teachers to bring their classes to your sale? How will you do that?

- Are you going to use your classroom for the sale? How will you arrange the desks and chairs? Do you need to make any signs to use in the room? How will you organize the items if you have a garage sale?

- If you are going to make something, where and when will you make it?

- What day will you have your sale?

Make a Schedule and Assign Tasks

1. Get a calendar or a sheet of paper. Assign days and deadlines for all the tasks you listed.

2. Decide which tasks will be done in school and which tasks will be done at home or after school.

3. Assign workers to perform the tasks. List them on the schedule. (Some tasks can be accomplished by small groups.) You may want to pick a project manager. The *manager* makes sure people complete their tasks on time. This is your volunteer project. Your teacher should not be in charge.

Day of the Sale Plan

1. Decide what tasks have to be performed on the day of the sale. This includes set-up, the sale itself, and clean-up.

2. Decide which workers you will need on the sale day. For example, if you prepare food that day, how many people are needed to prepare and package it? (Your teacher may explain what "mass production" is and help you organize assembly lines to produce your project.) You will need a cashier or two. You may need baggers. Assign workers.

3. Make a schedule for Day of Sale tasks and workers.

After the Sale

1. Add the money you made. Subtract your expenses and pay your bills if you have any. What's left is your profit.

2. Decide how you will give your profit to the group you selected. For example, will you write a letter or present it in person? If you are going to buy something for your school, who will purchase it?

We Need You!—Finding Volunteer Work for Young People

In *Dream Catchers,* you learned about volunteer work Sometimes people volunteer to help people they know, and sometimes people volunteer to help people they don't know. Sometimes people volunteer for a good cause, like collecting donations to fight cancer or earning money to buy computers for your school. Most communities have volunteer work younger people can do. Sometimes it's in hospitals or working at a local shelter or food bank. Churches, synagogues, mosques, and other religious groups often have programs which require volunteers. Your job is to find a volunteer opportunity for someone your age.

Directions

Find one volunteer program where you live that could use the services of people your age. Your parent(s), guardian(s), or teacher can help you. Call or visit the program to get information on the topics listed below.

Ask the following questions:

- What do you need volunteers to do? Describe as many different opportunities as are available.

- How many days a week or month do volunteers usually work?

- Do you need volunteers on specific days or times? Which days and what time?

- Could someone volunteer after school or on weekends?

- Where will volunteers work?

- Do volunteers need any special skills?

- Could friends volunteer and work together?

- Do you provide transportation for volunteers if needed?

Using the information you gather, write a "Want Ad" to explain the volunteer work. The class can create a "Volunteer Opportunities" bulletin board, and each person can post her or his "Want Ad" on it. Your ad should explain:

- The Work: Describe what a volunteer would do and if friends can volunteer together.

- Skills: Explain the skills that might be needed.

- Location: Give the address, phone number, and a contact person's name.

- Day(s) and Time(s): Give all possible days, times, and any other important information.

- Transportation: Explain how the volunteer can get to and from the location.

©JIST Works

Write a Letter Home—Part I

You have now finished Part 1 of *Dream Catchers*. Write a letter home explaining what you have learned. You can use your book for help.

Directions

Write a letter home. Use the suggestions given below. Your teacher will explain the correct letter form. You also can look up rules for writing letters in your language book. If you mail the letter, address the envelope correctly.

Include the following information in your letter:

- **Paragraph 1**—Give the title of your book and the section title for Part 1. (Check your language book for the correct way to write book titles and chapter titles.) Explain that you have just finished all the activities in Part 1.

- **Paragraph 2**—Explain that you learned jobs can be grouped together in different ways. Explain what career clusters are. Tell which cluster(s) interests you the most. (The ones you might like to work in someday.) You might even give the job titles of some jobs you liked.

- **Paragraph 3**—Explain that you learned jobs can also be grouped by who or what you work with (People and Animals, Things and Machinery, and Data and Ideas). Explain what working conditions are. Tell which of these groups interest you the most.

- **Paragraph 4**—Tell what you learned about volunteer work. Explain how you studied all the work it takes to run a home.

- **Paragraph 5**—Explain which activity you liked the most in Part 1 and why.

Extra Activity

Letter Exchange

Exchange letters with a classmate. Proofread one another's letter. Make sure they are written in the correct form. Check for spelling errors and punctuation. Write a final, corrected copy of your letter.

Part 2

The Stuff Dreams Are Made Of—Discovering Your Skills

Make a Skills Chain

In *Dream Catchers,* you learned that skills are like building blocks. One skill is made up of many other skills you have learned. Often, you must be able to do one skill in order to do the next.

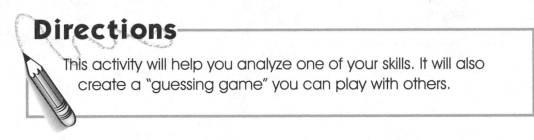

Directions

This activity will help you analyze one of your skills. It will also create a "guessing game" you can play with others.

1. Select a skill you have. (It can be anything: rowing a boat, throwing a ball, writing poetry, or painting your bedroom.) Write the skill on a separate sheet of paper. Underneath your skill, write all the other skills (let's call these sub-skills) you had to learn to do the skill. Put the sub-skills in the order that you learned them. (For example, you had to learn alphabet letters before you could learn the sounds for each letter.)

Materials Needed

■ Scissors

■ Construction paper

■ Glue

■ Pen or black marker

2. Cut the construction paper in strips about 1 inch wide and 3 inches long. You will need one paper strip for each sub-skill.

3. Write your sub-skills on the paper strips. Put one sub-skill on each strip. Your paper strips will be glued into a circle to make a chain "link." Be sure to write your sub-skill large enough so it can be read after you make your link.

4. Make your skills chain. Glue your first skill strip in a circle to make your first link. Glue the next skill strip around the first link to begin making a chain. Continue making links until your chain is complete. Make sure your links are in the right order. DO NOT include a link that names your skill.

5. Give your chain to a classmate to read. See if the classmate can guess your skill. Trade your chain with several classmates.

Extra Activity

Link Your Skills

After playing the "guessing game," add a link to the chain that names your skill. Hang the chains to decorate your classroom. Or you can make one long chain from everyone's chains. This will show what a skilled class you are! Hang the long chain in your classroom.

Make a Skills Bank

Some people use banks to save money. Maybe you even have a bank to save your allowance. A bank is a place to store something valuable. It doesn't have to be money.

Directions

This activity is about another kind of bank—a skills bank. It will help you to see all the skills you are learning. It also will show you how valuable your skills are. Follow the steps below.

1. Cut a slot in the top of your shoe box or coffee can lid. Make the slot large enough to insert folded pieces of paper.

2. Use the unlined paper to cover your box or can. Cut it to the size you need.

3. Write "My Skills Bank" and your name on the cover. Decorate the paper with crayons or markers. Add any other decorations you want.

4. Glue the paper to your can or box.

How to Use Your Skills Bank

Once or twice a week, put skills in your bank (maybe every Monday and Friday). Write each skill on a piece of paper, fold it, and put it in your bank. You can put in any skills you've learned inside or outside of school. For example, when you finish a chapter in a book, write a summary of what you've learned.

After several weeks, open your skills bank and read all your skills. You may want to record them in a "New Skills Notebook." Then start saving your skills again.

Share Your Skills

In *Dream Catchers,* you learned that you have lots of skills. It's fun to share your skills with others. This activity suggests ways to share skills.

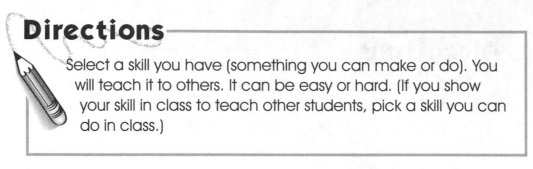

Directions

Select a skill you have (something you can make or do). You will teach it to others. It can be easy or hard. (If you show your skill in class to teach other students, pick a skill you can do in class.)

1. Write instructions on how to do your skill. Follow the steps below to write clear questions:

    ●   Give your instructions a title. The title must clearly state what the instructions are for, for example, "How to Make a Paper Airplane," or "How to Play Cat's Cradle," or "How to Jump Rope Double Dutch."

    ●   List all the tools or materials needed (if any) to follow the instructions. Put them under a heading "Tools and Materials Needed."

    ●   Give all instructions in step-by-step order. Number each step. Each step should give only one instruction.

    ●   Each instruction should begin with a command word like "fold," "cut," "bend," "write," etc.

2. Draw illustrations if needed to make your instructions clearer.

Extra Activity

Skills Demonstrations

1. Plan a "skills hour" once a week where classmates can show their skills. Pass out copies of your instructions if people want them.

2. Exchange instructions with classmates. See if they can do the skill by following the instructions. (If they can't, the author may need to change the instructions.)

3. Invite another class to your room for a "Skills Fair." Have several skills demonstrations take place in different areas in the classroom. Let your visitors watch different demonstrations.

You Can Be an Apprentice

People can learn job-related skills as apprentices. *Apprentices* work under a skilled worker who trains them to do the job. Apprentices learn by doing the work with help from the trainer.

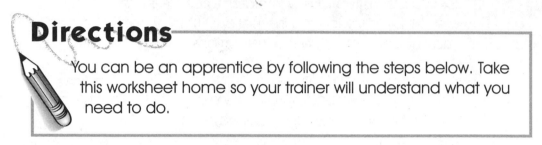

Directions

You can be an apprentice by following the steps below. Take this worksheet home so your trainer will understand what you need to do.

1. Have someone outside of school teach you how to do something new. It can be anything—how to cook an egg, iron a shirt, use a drill, change the oil in the car, or knit. Explain to your trainer that you want to learn a new skill. The trainer can help you select one.

2. Your trainer will show you how to do the new skill. The trainer may make you watch first, before you try it on your own. Or he or she may guide you through the steps as you try it the first time.

3. Keep practicing your new skill until you can do it correctly by yourself without any help. When you have mastered the skill, you are no longer an apprentice. Now you are a skilled worker.

4. Keep an "Apprentice Journal" of the learning process. Write down what you did as you learned your new skill. What mistakes did you make? What was hard? What was easy? What was fun? What was not fun? How long did it take to master your skill?

5. When you have mastered your skill, have your trainer sign and date your journal. Now you are a skilled worker!

Extra Activity

What's Your Story?

You can share your new skill with your classmates by turning your journal writings into a story. Draw illustrations too. Maybe you can do an "Apprentice Bulletin Board" with stories from the whole class.

Practice Makes Perfect

You've probably heard the old saying, "Practice makes perfect." One reason we have "old sayings" is because they are usually true! This activity will help you discover if "practice *does* make perfect."

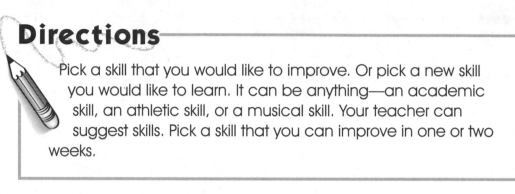

Directions

Pick a skill that you would like to improve. Or pick a new skill you would like to learn. It can be anything—an academic skill, an athletic skill, or a musical skill. Your teacher can suggest skills. Pick a skill that you can improve in one or two weeks.

1. Set up a goal sheet for yourself. Include the following information:

   - Describe your goal. What skill do you want to master?

   - Plan a practice schedule. Write down 1) how much time each day, 2) how many days a week, and 3) how many weeks you will practice.

   - Describe what you will do when you practice.

2. Keep a practice journal. Describe your activities. How long did you actually practice? What did you do? Do you feel that you improved your skill?

3. When the time is up (one or two weeks), answer these questions in your journal: Does "practice make perfect"? Did you really improve? Do you feel you've mastered your skill? Do you need more practice? If you didn't improve, why not?

Extra Activity

Share Your Answers

Share your experience with other students in your class. Read your journal to them. See how other people answered the questions in #3 above.

What Academic Skills Are Needed for Jobs?

In your *Dream Catchers,* you read stories that showed why people need academic skills for their jobs. How important are academic skills? This activity will show you.

Directions

Interview someone to learn how people use school subjects on the job. To do your interview, follow the instructions below.

1. Select an adult you know to interview.

2. Ask the following questions. Be sure to take good notes on what is said. Because different jobs use different academic skills, you will get some "No" answers.

   - What is your job?

   - Do you read on your job? What do you read?

   - Do you write on your job? What kinds of writing do you do?

   - Do you have to talk with others on your job? What kind of talking does your job require?

   - Do you use math on your job? How do you use it?

   - Do you use scientific information on your job? What do you use? How do you use it?

   - Do you use social studies on your job? (This includes history, geography, government, information on other cultures or people, and so forth.) What information do you use?

   - Do you need a foreign language for your job? What language? How do you use it?

3. When you are done, use your notes to write a report. Call it "Using Academic Skills at Work." Share your report with the class.

Extra Activity

List the Results

Make big lists from the results of all interviews. Do a list of each academic skill. For example, make a list called "Reading at Work." Then write down all the different kinds of reading people do at work. Make separate lists for all academic subjects: writing, talking, math, science, social studies, and foreign languages. Hang your lists in the classroom.

Using Your Academic Skills Outside of School

Think about all the things you do outside school. Do you use academic skills when you're not in school? Let's find out.

Directions

Write the academic skills you need to do the activities below. Don't leave any skills out—your job could depend on it!

1. Make lemonade to sell.

   Skills used: _____

   _____

2. Make signs advertising my product.

   Skills used: _____

   _____

3. Make change when customers buy lemonade.

   Skills used: _____

   _____

4. Figure out my profits.

   Skills used: _____

   _____

I've Cut My Hand!

Suppose you fell and cut your hand. Then you went inside and washed the cut. Next, you put antiseptic on the cut. Finally, you put a band-aid over the cut.

Why did you clean and bandage your cut? What have you learned in school that taught you cleaning a wound is important? Write your answer on the lines below.

_____

_____

_____

_____

_____

_____

_____

Activity Sheet #44
Individual activity

Using Your Self-Management Skills

In *Dream Catchers,* you learned about *self-management* skills. They included personal qualities like:

- **Good Work Habits**—A work habit is the way you do your work. Good work habits include qualities like following directions, getting work done on time, working quickly and neatly, and being prepared.

- **Good Work Attitudes**—A work attitude is how you feel about doing your work. Good work attitudes include qualities like being eager to try new tasks, working independently, sticking with hard tasks, being cheerful, accepting responsibility, and obeying rules.

- **Good Interpersonal Skills**—Interpersonal skills are how you get along with other people when doing work. Good interpersonal skills include qualities like cooperating, sharing, accepting others, respecting others, respecting authority, and being honest.

Directions

Use notebook paper to write a story about a time when you used good self-management skills. It could be a school assignment, a chore at home, a project for scouts, or playing on a team. Try to name all the good work habits, good work attitudes, and interpersonal skills you used.

Improving Your Self-Management Skills

In "What Are Self-Management Skills?" in *Dream Catchers,* you gave yourself "marks" on your self-management skills. Look at any "I" or "X" marks you have. These are the areas that need improvement—starting now!

Directions

To get better, you need to set goals for improvement. The steps below will help you set goals.

1. Select one self-management skill to improve. Write it on the chart on the next page.

2. List five rules that will help you improve this skill. Write them on the chart.

3. Tape this chart to the inside top of your desk or keep it in a notebook.

4. Each week for four weeks, grade yourself on how you followed your rules. Use the marking system on your chart. Put your grade in the box at the bottom of your chart. If you don't improve in four weeks, review your rules and start again.

Self-Management Skills Improvement Chart

Skill I Will Improve:			

Rules I Will Follow to Improve This Skill:

1.

2.

3.

4.

5.

Grade Yourself	Week #1	Week #2	Week #3	Week #4
0 = Outstanding				
S = Satisfactory				
I = Improvement				
X = Unsatisfactory				

Using Time Efficiently in the Workplace

Using time efficiently is a very important work habit. To be *efficient* means you get your work done quickly, but you still do a good job.

Directions

Read Maria's story below to see why efficient workers are so important. Then solve the problems that come after the story.

Maria's House Painting Business

Maria owns Pronto Painting Company. Her company paints houses. George Liska wants Pronto Painting Company to paint his house. Maria has to decide what to charge Mr. Liska. She judges how many hours it will take to paint his house. Then she figures out what her expenses will be to paint it. Maria has to pay salaries to her workers to paint the house. That is her biggest expense. Maria subtracts the expenses from what she will charge Mr. Liska. The money left over is her profit. She uses her profit to pay herself and to keep her business running. Maria figures out her profit by using a worksheet. Look at her worksheet below.

Expense and Profit Worksheet

Expenses:

Total number of hours needed to paint house	64 hours
Salaries for two painters at $10 per hour	
(64 x $10 = $640)	$640.00
Other Expenses:	+ 100.00
Total Expenses:	$ 740.00

Profit:

Charge to Mr. Liska to paint house	$1,200.00
Less Total Expenses:	− 740.00
Total Profit:	$ 460.00

Can Wasting Time Waste Money?

A *cost over run* in business is when something costs more than you thought it would. Maria thought it would take 64 hours to paint Mr. Liska's house. What would happen if her painters wasted time? Suppose they took a lot of breaks, forgot their tools and had to get them, and just worked slowly? What would happen if they took 74 hours to finish the painting instead of 64 hours at $10 per hour? How much money would Maria lose? Figure out her loss below:

1. Estimated profit from Maria's worksheet $460.00

    Cost over run (10 more hours × $10.00 per hour)   _____

    Actual profit   _____

2. The cost over run on Mr. Liska's house was $100. Suppose Maria's company had 10 jobs in one month. If each job had a cost over run of $100, how much money would her company lose in a month? $_____

3. Maria's company works 12 months a year. What if she had a cost over run of $1,000 for 7 months in a year. How much money would her company lose in a year? $_____

4. Do you think wasting time wastes money? Why?

    _____

    _____

5. If you were Maria, how would you solve the problem of your painters working too slowly?

    _____

    _____

6. What does it mean to be an efficient worker?

    _____

    _____

One of the top three reasons people get fired from their jobs is because they don't use their work time efficiently!

Make a School Time Card

Using time efficiently is very important at work. Many business activities are connected to time. Lots of people have jobs that use time cards, which keep track of the hours people work. Often, people even put their time cards in a machine that marks the time they get to work and the time they leave. If a worker gets to work at 8:01 a.m. instead of 8 a.m., the time card shows he or she was late!

Directions

All businesses want workers who always get to work on time and don't miss work. To track how you use time, follow the instructions below.

1. Make a time card on an index card.

2. Put your name and the dates for one week (Monday through Friday) at the top of your time card. For example: Kate Lindsay, November 20-25, 2006.

3. Make two columns underneath your name and date. One should say "Time In." The other should say "Time Out."

4. Write the days of the week along the left-hand margin for Monday through Friday.

5. Make an envelope to keep your time card in. Fold a piece of paper in half. The fold will be the top. Tape the sides and bottom of the paper to your desk. (The inside top would be a good place.) Keep your time card in the envelope.

6. Your teacher will tell you a time when all students have to be at their desks in the morning ready to work. For example: 9:00 a.m.

7. At 9:00 a.m., your teacher will say, "Sign in please." If you are at your desk, put "9:00" under the "Time In" column. If you are not at your desk ready to sign in, write "Late."

8. Follow the same procedure for signing out. If you leave class early, write the time in the "Time Out" column.

9. If you are absent, make sure to mark absent on your time card when you return to school.

10. At the end of the week, make a record of the number of times you were on time, late, left early, and absent. Make a new time card for the next week. Use your time card for a whole grading period (or the whole year). Then you will know if you are a reliable worker.

The Case of the "Bad Worker"

Not all workers have good work habits, attitudes, or interpersonal skills. Working with a person who has bad self-management skills affects everyone. Have you ever worked with a person who wouldn't cooperate or didn't do his or her fair share of the work? You know that wasn't fun. To find out how "bad workers" can affect other workers, do the activity below.

Directions

Pick someone you know who works at a part- or full-time job. Ask the following questions. Take careful notes of the person's answers.

1. Did you ever have to work with someone who did not have good work habits, attitudes, or interpersonal skills?

2. What bad work habits, attitudes, or interpersonal skills did this person display?

3. How did her or his behavior affect other workers?

4. Did anyone ever try to "correct" this bad behavior? What happened?

Extra Activity

Write a Report

Use your notes to write a report about the "bad worker." Share your report with your classmates.

What Job-Related Skills Do You Need?

In *Dream Catchers*, you learned that workers need special skills to do their jobs. These are called *job-related* skills. In this activity, you will interview someone you know. The interview will help you learn more about the job-related skills.

Directions

Select an adult to interview. Ask the following questions. Be sure to take good notes on what is said.

1. What is your job? _____

2. What special skills do you need to do this work? Name and describe some of these skills. _____

_____

_____

_____

3. Where did you learn the skills for your job? _____

_____

_____

4. Can the skills for your job be learned in other places too? _____
What are the other places? _____

_____

_____

_____

5. Does your job require any kind of academic degree? _____

    What kind of degree? _____

    _____

    _____

    _____

6. Does your job require a special license? Did you have to pass a test to get

    your license? _____

    _____

    _____

    _____

7. Do you have to keep learning new skills for your job? _____

    Where do you learn them? _____

    _____

    _____

    _____

    _____

    _____

Extra Activity

Write a Report

Use your interview notes to write a report called "The Job-Related Skills of a _____." (Fill in the job title.) Share your report with your classmates.

Create a Job-Related Skills Bulletin Board

In *Dream Catchers,* you learned about job-related skills. They are special skills workers need to do their jobs. Different jobs require different kinds of skills. This activity will show the different kinds of skills.

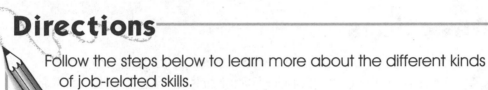

Directions

Follow the steps below to learn more about the different kinds of job-related skills.

1. Cut pictures from magazines of people working at different jobs. You also can draw pictures.

2. For each job, make a list of all the skills needed for the job. You might like to do this in a small group. Give your list a title, for example, "Job Skills Used by a Nurse."

3. Proofread your list. Make sure all words are spelled correctly. Copy the list over if necessary. Make sure it's neat.

4. Paste the picture of the job and the job skills list on a piece of construction paper or poster board.

5. Decorate your bulletin boards or the walls outside your classroom with your work.

Using Want Ads to Learn About Skills

Every day, newspapers contain "want ads." These ads are put in the paper by employers who want to hire people. The want ads list the skills employers look for in workers.

Directions

The Sunday newspaper usually has the largest want ad section. Bring the Sunday want ads to class to do this activity. Follow the steps below to discover what skills employers want.

1. Divide the wants ads among small groups in your class. Each group might take one page. Or divide the ads alphabetically.

2. Each group will need four sheets of notebook paper. Label the first sheet "Academic Skills," the second "Self-Management Skills," the third "Job-Related Skills," and the fourth "Training or Education Required."

3. Read your group's want ads. Every time you find an academic, self-management, or job-related skill, or specific education or training required, write it on the paper with that heading.

4. When all groups have finished, compare what you have discovered about skills and training.

Extra Activity

Skills and Training List

You can combine each group's list into one long list for each category. Display your lists in the classroom.

©JIST Works

Write a Letter Home—Part 2

You now have finished Part 2 of your *Dream Catchers* book. Write a letter home explaining what you have learned. You can use *Dream Catchers* for help.

Directions

Write a letter home using the suggestions given below. Your teacher will explain the correct letter form. You also can look up letter writing rules in your language book. If you mail the letter, address the envelope correctly.

Your letter should include the following information:

- **Paragraph 1**—Explain that you have just finished all the activities in Part 2 of your book. Give Part 2's title and tell what Part 2 was about.

- **Paragraph 2**—Explain what academic, self-management, and job-related skills are. You might give some examples of each. Also tell how academic and self-management skills are important for both school and work.

- **Paragraph 3**—Explain that you learned about different ways to get education and training for jobs. You might give a few examples. Tell what kind of training or education interests you.

- **Paragraph 4**—Explain which activity you liked the most in Part 2 and why.

Extra Activity

Letter Exchange

Exchange letters with a classmate. Proofread one another's letter. Make sure they are written in the correct form. Check for punctuation and spelling errors. Write a final, corrected copy of your letter.

Part 3

Making Dreams Come True—Ability, Effort, and Achievement

Produce a "Three Little Pigs" Play

Dream Catchers contains the story "A Modern Fable of the Three Little Pigs." Changing the story into a play to perform would be fun! Read the instructions to see how to do it.

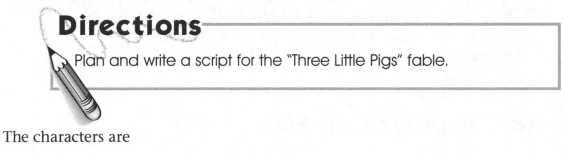

Directions

Plan and write a script for the "Three Little Pigs" fable.

The characters are

- Narrator
- Pig I Did It
- Pig I Can
- The Big Bad Wolf
- Pig I'll Try
- Mother Pig

You can change the whole story into a script, or you can just decide what parts of the story the narrator will read. Then let the characters make up what they will say based on the story as they perform it. (That's called *extemporaneous theatre*.) Plan and make costumes. (You can make great pig and wolf masks from brown paper bags.) Plan and make scenery, but keep it simple.

Extra Activity

Perform Pig Plays

1. If you and your classmates wrote "Which Little Pig Are You?" stories in your *Dream Catchers* book, pick the best story for each little pig. (You can select students to be judges or your teacher can pick them.) Turn those stories into plays, too. You can divide your class into four groups. Each group can plan and perform a play.

2. Invite other classes to your "Pig Theatre." Perform the plays for them. Do "A Modern Fable of Three Little Pigs" first. Then do the "Which Little Pig Are You?" plays next. You can have your audience guess which little pig was shown in the play.

You Can Improve Too!

Directions

Pick a subject you identified as a weakness. (See "Know Your Strengths and Weaknesses" in *Dream Catchers*.) Then fill in the chart below. Try to be specific with your solutions. For example: **Causes of My Problem**—"I forgot to take my books home." **How I Can Improve**—"Write down the books I need in an assignment notebook."

My Work Improvement Plan

Name: _____

I need to improve in (name subject): _____

Causes of My Problem	How I Can Improve

80

My Time Journal

Date:			
6:00 a.m.		6:30	
7:00		7:30	
8:00		8:30	
9:00		9:30	
10:00		10:30	
11:00		11:30	
12:00 p.m.		12:30 p.m.	
1:00		1:30	
2:00		2:30	
3:00		3:30	
4:00		4:30	
5:00		5:30	
6:00		6:30	
7:00		7:30	
8:00		8:30	
9:00		9:30	
10:00		10:30	
11:00		11:30	
12:00 a.m.			

Time Spent on My Weekly Activities

Time Spent on My Weekly Activities (Example)

Activity	Total Weekly Hours
Going to school	35
Eating	10½
Doing something outside	9
Working a paper route	5
Walking the dog	3½
Doing chores	2½
Watching TV or movies	12
Playing video games	10
Sleeping	58
Talking on the phone	2½
Going to church	2
Doing homework	3½
Reading for fun (not for school)	2
Doing personal care activities such as showering and dressing	5

Time Spent on My Weekly Activities

Activity	Total Weekly Hours

How You Use Your Time

For your "Time Journal" (see "Managing Your Study Time" in *Dream Catchers*), you grouped all your week's activities and added the hours you spent on each activity. Many times in business, people put information on charts and graphs. That makes comparing information easier. Use the information to make a bar chart of your activities and the time you spent on them.

Directions

At the top of each column on the graph, write the names of your different activities—for example, "Eating," "Studying," "Watching TV," and so forth. Use a marker to draw a bar up to the number of hours you spent on the activity. Use a different color for each activity.

Activities:

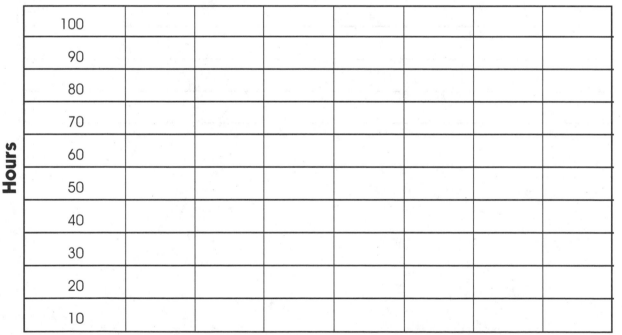

Hours							
100							
90							
80							
70							
60							
50							
40							
30							
20							
10							

©JIST Works

Setting Achievement Goals

You know a lot now about your weaknesses and how you spend your time. You can use that knowledge to improve your school work. Use your "Work Improvement Plan" and your "Time Journal" to help set achievement goals.

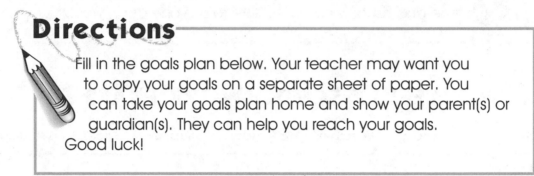

Directions

Fill in the goals plan below. Your teacher may want you to copy your goals on a separate sheet of paper. You can take your goals plan home and show your parent(s) or guardian(s). They can help you reach your goals. Good luck!

My Achievement Goals

Goal 1: My study time during the week will be between _____ and _____.

Goal 2: My quiet place to study will be _____.

Goal 3: On weekends, I will study on _____ (day or days). I will study between _____ and _____.

Goal 4: I will spend the most time on the following subjects. These are my weaknesses. _____.

Goal 5: On weekdays, I plan to be in bed each night with the lights out by _____.

Goal 6: I will only watch TV and movies, play video games, or surf the Web for _____ hour(s) on weekdays and _____ hour(s) on weekends.

Make a Schoolwork Planner

Directions

Use the "Weekly Schoolwork Planner" below to organize your time and schoolwork. Make sure to use one each week.

MY WEEKLY SCHOOLWORK PLANNER

Activity	Monday	Tuesday	Wednesday	Thursday	Friday	Weekend
Books and Supplies to Bring Home						
Work Due Tomorrow						
Upcoming Tests						
Subjects to Review						
Times to Study						
Other Things I Have to Do Today						

Managing Your School Study Time

Sometimes you get time during the school day to study. Do you use that time efficiently? Do you get your work done in the time your teacher gives you?

Directions

Take the quiz below to find out how you manage your study time at school. Answer each question and read the answer key to find out your score.

MANAGING YOUR SCHOOL STUDY TIME QUIZ

Statement	Yes	No
1. It usually takes me at least five minutes to get my materials (for example, book, paper, and pencil) together to start studying.	❑	❑
2. I frequently need to borrow paper or a pencil from classmates before I start studying.	❑	❑
3. My desk is a mess most of the time.	❑	❑
4. I often sharpen my pencil during study time.	❑	❑
5. Sometimes I write notes to my friends during study time.	❑	❑
6. I look at the clock or my watch at least four times when I'm studying.	❑	❑
7. I often think, "I'll just take this home and do it" instead of getting my work done in school.	❑	❑
8. I like to talk with people sitting near me while I'm studying.	❑	❑
9. I like to look out the window during study time.	❑	❑
10. I always seem to be rushing to get my work done.	❑	❑
11. I like to read other things during study time instead of doing my assignment.	❑	❑

Answer Key: *Did you have more than four "Yes" answers? Then you need to use your school study time more efficiently. Use Activity Sheet #61 to set study goals for school.*

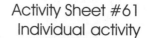

Using School Study Time Better

Your "Managing Your School Study Time" quiz (Activity Sheet #60) helped you identify weaknesses in your study habits. Look over all your "Yes" answers. Decide how you are wasting time. Follow the instructions below to turn your weaknesses into strengths.

Directions

Set three goals on the chart below to help improve your study skills. Tape your goal plan in a place where you can easily see it. When you have study time at school, quickly read your goals. When study time is over, ask yourself if you used your time well.

MY SCHOOL STUDY TIME GOALS

Goal #1:
Goal #2:
Goal #3:

"A Test Is Coming!"

A test grade often shows how carefully you studied for a test. Do you study the "right" things? Do you plan your study time wisely? Do you have all the materials you need to study? Do you follow your teacher's instructions? Do you spend enough time studying?

Directions

Work in small groups to brainstorm good ways to prepare for tests. Follow the steps below to create a worksheet to help you study.

1. Make a list of all the different things you should do to study for a test. Your list should apply to all your subjects. Put down everything you can possibly think of at first.

2. Read your list. See if you can put the different items into categories (like putting things in clusters). Reading, reviewing, and materials might be some of your clusters.

3. Organize your clusters in order of their importance. What is the most important thing to do? What is second, third, or fourth?

4. Organize the items in your clusters in order of their importance. Now you may choose to throw out some of your items or combine them.

5. Compare your group's clusters with other groups. Add anything to your list that other groups had on their lists, but your group didn't. If groups have different priorities, discuss those differences and decide who is "right."

6. Write a final copy of your clusters and their items in priority order. Make it a worksheet checklist. Then students using your worksheet to study for a test can check off the items as they finish them.

7. See if someone in your group can type your checklist. Have your teacher run off copies for everyone. Use your checklist every time you have a test.

Learn from Your Mistakes

Imagine that you are looking at a glass that is half filled with water. How would you describe the glass of water? Would you say it is "half empty" or "half full"? "Half empty" is a negative way of looking at things and "half full" is positive.

If you took a test and got half the questions wrong, you'd get a very bad grade. But the positive side is that you also got half the questions right! If you got half of the questions right, you can get more right next time.

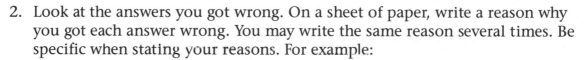

Directions

This activity will help you check your test-taking skills. You CAN improve your test grades! Follow the steps below.

1. When you get a test back, look up the right answers for answers that were wrong. Correct your test. If it's a math test, redo the problems to get the right answers.

2. Look at the answers you got wrong. On a sheet of paper, write a reason why you got each answer wrong. You may write the same reason several times. Be specific when stating your reasons. For example:

   - I was careless answering the question. (You knew the right answer but marked it wrong on the test.)
   - I misunderstood the question.
   - I didn't study that part of the chapter.
   - I didn't know how to do the problem.
   - I forgot the answer.

3. Look at the reasons why you made mistakes on your test. Which reason did you give the most? That's the area to improve when studying and taking tests.

4. Write some tips for yourself to avoid making these mistakes. You can use the lines below. For example, if you said, "I was careless," your rule might be, "Read test questions carefully and check my answers when I'm finished." You might add these rules to your "A Test Is Coming!" checklist. If they're already on the checklist, put a star by them to remind you to really work on those study skills. Use your new knowledge every time you study for a test. Review your tips before taking a test.

My Tips for Taking a Test

1. _____

_____

2. _____

_____

3. _____

_____

4. _____

_____

5. _____

_____

6. _____

_____

7. _____

_____

8. _____

_____

9. _____

_____

My Workplace Plan

Directions

Fill in the blanks below to design your study workplace. Take your plan home. Show it to your parent(s) or guardian(s). They can help you organize and use your workplace.

1. Where will I work? (You need a desk or table, good lighting, and a quiet place.)

   _____

2. What supplies will I need? (List everything you should have for all subjects.)

   _____

   _____

   _____

3. Where will I keep my supplies? (A desk drawer is great. A shoe box or some other container also will work. Plan a place to keep your supplies.)

   _____

   _____

4. How can I remember to bring home the books I need?

   _____

   _____

   _____

5. What study rules should I follow? (You need quiet time with no interruptions from people, the phone, or TV to concentrate best. Get snacks before you start.) Write your rules.

_____

_____

_____

_____

_____

_____

_____

6. Who will I study with? (Most of the time, it's more efficient to study alone. List the times when it would be OK to study with friends.)

_____

_____

_____

_____

_____

_____

_____

Organizing an Efficient Workplace

Sometimes *where* you work can make you an inefficient worker. (*Inefficient* is the opposite of efficient.) A well-organized workplace is also important on a job. Businesses want workplaces where workers won't waste time getting their work done. Sometimes they even hire special people called *consultants* to design the most efficient workplace possible. Read Willy's story below. It shows that *where* you work can make a difference.

Can You Help Willy?

The Richards family owns a doughnut shop. Willy Richards comes in at 4:00 a.m. every day to make the doughnuts. Willy loves his work, but he is unhappy with his kitchen. He thinks the way the kitchen is organized wastes time. Willy has to work long hours. Wasting time cuts down on the profit the doughnut shop earns. Willy decides he wants to change the kitchen. He wants a more efficient workplace. Then he can make the doughnuts in less time, which means more profit for the family.

Directions

All the steps to make doughnuts are listed here. The next page shows you a floor plan of Willy's kitchen. Look at the floor plan. Pretend you are Willy. Go through each step to make the doughnuts. You can draw arrows or footsteps on the floor plan to show all the walking Willy has to do. Does Willy waste time walking back and forth?

Steps for Making Doughnuts

1. Get the following items and bring them to the work table:
   - baking supplies (flour, sugar, etc.)
   - baking utensils (bowls, spoons, etc.)
   - milk

2. Mix the batter for the doughnuts on the work table.

3. Take the batter to the doughnut maker and pour it in.

4. Get the baking pans and bring them to the doughnut maker. Make doughnuts.

5. Put doughnuts in the oven.

6. Take baked doughnuts out of the oven and put them on the cooling racks.

7. Bring cooled doughnuts to the work table to frost them.

8. Put all dirty baking utensils and pans in the sink when done.

Floor Plan of Willy's Kitchen

Refrigerator	Sink	Oven
Baking Supplies		Work Table
Doughnut Maker		
Baking Utensils		
Cooling Racks	Rack of Clean Baking Pans	Door

You Can Be Willy's Consultant

Directions

Get a blank sheet of paper and a ruler. Draw a 5x6-inch rectangle. Draw a new floor plan for Willy's kitchen. Help him save time. You might try several plans before you get the best design. The floor plan should include: 1) a place for baking supplies; 2) a place for baking utensils; 3) a sink; 4) a refrigerator; 5) a work table; 6) a doughnut maker; 7) an oven; 8) a place for clean baking pans; and 9) cooling racks.

You can do this activity in small groups. Compare your floor plans to other plans. Vote on which one is the best. You also could set up each group's kitchen design in the classroom. Use desks as the kitchen furniture. Then you could actually count the steps needed in each plan to see which one is the best.

Improving Your School Workplace

Dream Catchers had an activity to improve the organization of your workplace at home. But the classroom and your desk are also your workplace. Your class and teacher can analyze the schoolroom workplace. Think of ways to improve it.

Directions

Select one day to be your "Workplace Analysis" day. Think of ways to improve the efficiency of your classroom workplace. Brainstorm in small groups. Write answers to the suggestions listed below. Then discuss your suggestions as a class. Establish workplace rules and policies. All businesses have them.

1. **Your desk**—Your desk is personal. Everyone will not organize his or her desk in the same way. Yet, try to think of some general rules for keeping books and supplies easy to get to. Also, consider how often and when desks should be cleaned.

2. **Old homework papers, worksheets, and tests**—These papers are good sources for study and test review, but most students throw them away or lose them. Develop a classroom filing system. Then everyone has a place to file and save papers. Keeping track of paperwork is extremely important in businesses.

3. **Desk arrangement**—How are your desks arranged? Is the arrangement good for getting work done? Can you think of different arrangements to make your classroom a more efficient place to work?

4. **Seat arrangements**—How are seats assigned? Do you constantly talk to the people sitting next to you? Can you sit near your friends and not talk to them? What might be the best way to assign seats?

5. **Quiet time**—Certain times during the day may be used as "quiet time" for study, homework, or reading. How should "quiet time" be announced? Should you have a sign or signal like ringing a bell? What rules should be followed during "quiet time"? For example, can you sharpen your pencil? What should happen to classmates who do not follow "quiet time" rules? People who do not follow the rules often get fired at work. They disrupt the efficiency of other workers.

6. **Rules and Policies**—First, set up your workplace rules and policies. Then review them every few months to see if they are working. If not, identify the problems and change your rules.

Developing a Job Chart

Every classroom has certain tasks that need to be done, such as cleaning the boards, watering plants, or feeding pets. Everyone in class should be responsible for doing tasks to keep the classroom orderly.

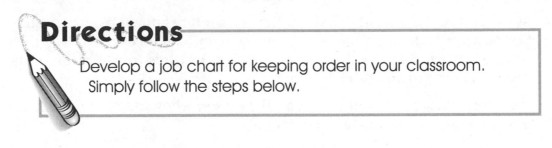

Directions

Develop a job chart for keeping order in your classroom. Simply follow the steps below.

1. In class discussion, make a list of all the tasks that need to be done each day and once a week.

2. Have one or two students volunteer to make a job chart for the classroom tasks. The job chart should contain

   - A "Supervisor" heading
   - A daily task list
   - A weekly task list

   Each task will have an index card with a student's name on it placed next to it. Be sure to leave enough space between each task for the card to fit.

3. Have a few students volunteer to write all students' names on index cards.

4. Hang your job chart on a bulletin board.

5. All students should take turns performing tasks in a rotating order. Follow the next set of steps to assign jobs.

Assigning Work

1. Put the index cards with the students' names on them in alphabetical order. Pin the first name next to "Supervisor" and pin other names next to each task. Store the remaining cards in a safe place.

2. The supervisor is responsible for checking to see that jobs are done. He or she also must do the job of anyone who is absent.

3. At the end of the day on Friday, the supervisor takes down the name cards. She or he puts them on the bottom of the name card deck. He or she then assigns new workers for the next week, takes the cards from the top of the deck, and pins them on the job chart.

4. If the supervisor is absent on Friday, the person whose name is next on the job chart will assign the next week's tasks.

Activity Sheet #68
Individual activity

Write a Letter Home—Part 3

You have now finished Part 3 of *Dream Catchers*. Write a letter home explaining what you have learned. You can use your book for help.

Directions

Write a letter home. Use the suggestions given below. Your teacher will explain the correct letter form. You also can look up letter writing rules in your language book. If you mail the letter, address the envelope correctly.

Your letter should include the following information:

- **Paragraph 1**—Explain that you have just finished all the activities in Part 3 of your *Dream Catchers* book. Give Part 3's title and tell what Part 3 was about.

- **Paragraph 2**—Explain that you have been learning ways to improve your study skills. Tell how you wrote a work improvement plan to help you improve in a subject (name the subject).

- **Paragraph 3**—Explain about your time journal and what you discovered about how you use your time. Explain that your time journal helped you establish study rules and achievement goals for yourself. You might give a few examples of your rules or goals.

- **Paragraph 4**—Explain what you learned about the relationship between ability, effort, and achievement.

- **Paragraph 5**—Tell which activity you liked best in Part 3 and why.

Extra Activity

Letter Exchange

Exchange letters with a classmate. Proofread one another's letter. Make sure they are written in the correct form. Check for punctuation and spelling errors. Write a final, corrected copy of your letter.

Part 4

Putting Your Dreams to Work—Work and the Needs and Functions of Society

Why Do People Work?

You might think the answer to that question is "for money." It's true that people do need money for food, shelter, and clothing. But if people only worked for money, everyone would try to get jobs that pay a lot. And all people don't do that. People also work because they like their jobs. Since people are different, what they like is different too. Follow the steps below to learn more about why people work.

Directions

You and your classmates are going to do a survey about why people work. Follow the steps below.

1. Ask your teacher this question: "What do you like about your work?" List three things in priority order. (The most important is #1.)

2. Each class member should ask five other people that question and bring the answers to class. (Remember that working at home is also a job.) Make sure to list the most important reason first. You might ask another teacher to see if his or her answer is different from your teacher's.

3. When your survey is done, make one big list of all the answers. Mark the number of times people gave an answer as their #1, #2, and #3 choice.

4. Bring your list to class. Combine all answers into one big list. The list will show all the different reasons people work. Hang the list on the bulletin board.

Job Satisfaction—What Do You Want?

In Activity #69—"Why Do People Work?"—your class made a list of all the reasons people work. You may have been surprised at the many different reasons given. Besides the need for money, people chose certain careers because they like the work. We call that "job satisfaction." What you do at work makes you feel good or satisfied.

Directions

Write a report about the kinds of job satisfaction you want from a career. Follow the steps below for help.

1. Read the list the class made of reasons people work.

2. Select the three reasons that would be most important to you. (You certainly may add any others that are not on the list.)

3. Write a few sentences about each one of your choices explaining why it is important to you.

4. Turn to the list of careers in your *Dream Catchers* book on pages 23–24. Select some careers you think might give the kind of job satisfaction you want. List the careers at the end of your report. Explain that these are jobs which might satisfy you.

Alternate Assignment

You may have done career research about one or more careers. You can pick one of those careers and explain why the work would give you job satisfaction. If you choose this option, make sure to explain what work activities a person would do on the job.

Why Do You Work?

Your "job" right now is to be a student and do your schoolwork. Do students have different reasons for doing their work just like adults on the job do? Find out by surveying your class.

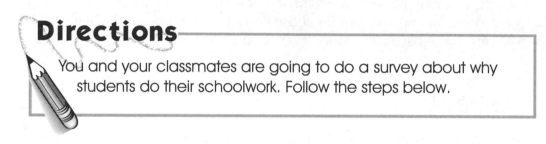

Directions

You and your classmates are going to do a survey about why students do their schoolwork. Follow the steps below.

1. On a sheet of paper, list in priority order (the most important first) all the reasons why you do your work in school. Write down as many as you can. Do not put your name on the paper.

2. Collect everyone's lists. Make one big class list of why students do their schoolwork. Mark the number of times students gave each reason as #1, #2, and #3.

3. Compare the students' reasons and the adults' reasons (from the survey in Activity #69) for doing work. Are some of the reasons the same? Which ones are different? Discuss your findings.

Work and Society

Although people have different jobs and different reasons for working, everyone's job is important. People in society depend on the work done by other people. For example, if a farmer didn't plant crops, we wouldn't have food to eat. Or if the refuse workers didn't collect the garbage, our environment would be messy and unhealthy. To show how people in society depend on one another to do their work, follow the instructions below.

Directions

You can do this activity alone or in small groups. You will select a product. Then you'll think of all the workers who helped get the product to you. Because nearly everyone wears cotton T-shirts, let's use that as our product.

1. Pretend that you just bought a cotton T-shirt with a design on the front. Make a list of all the workers you can think of who had a part in getting that product to you and their jobs. Brainstorm and write down as many jobs as you can.

2. Look at your list. Put the work in chronological order. (*Chronological* means to put in order by time: what had to be done first, second, etc.)

3. Get a big sheet of paper. Draw a big circle on it. You are going to make a pie chart to show the cycle of your product: what was done first, second, etc. Count the number of workers and jobs you have on your list. Divide your pie (the circle) into pieces. You should have a piece for each job on your list.

4. Working clockwise, write a worker and job in each pie piece. You can add illustrations if you have room.

5. Compare your pie chart to other groups' pie charts. See who thought of the most jobs and workers.

Extra Activity

Product Pie Chart

 Have each group select another product. Do a pie chart to show a product cycle from its beginning to when someone buys it. You might want to do some library research to help you list all the jobs involved.

Changes in Society and Work

One thing we can always count on is change. Our society today is vastly different from what it was like 100 years ago. We all know that. We sometimes don't realize, however, that society changes very quickly too. Ten years ago, no one had cell phones! Changes in society always affect the world of work. These changes may create the need for new jobs, more workers in a particular job, new products, or new businesses. The needs of society are always reflected in the workforce.

Directions

Below is a list of six recent changes in society. For each item below, write about how the changes in society caused changes in the world of work. For example, the change in #1 has caused a need for more "assisted living" apartments. This change, in turn, has caused a need for more nurses and nurses' aides. It has also caused a need for more in-home health care workers and day centers for elderly people. A day center for seniors is not only a new business; it needs workers to run it.

1. People are living longer and are more active in their older years.

2. More women work outside the home.

3. Many more jobs require education after high school.

4. Many people own personal computers and cell phones.

5. People don't have time to cook.

6. People are much more conscious about their health and keeping fit.

Extra Activity

Think of more recent changes in society or predict changes that will occur in the future. Write about how those changes affect the world of work.

The Changing Workforce— Jobs for Robots

Wouldn't you love to have a personal robot that could do all your chores for you—like clean your room, take out the garbage, or do the dishes? Robots are such a popular idea that many movies or TV shows about the future often have them as characters. Using robots to do work, however, is not just science fiction. Many businesses today use robots to do many different kinds of jobs. The science of developing robots is called *robotics*.

Directions

You are going to do research about the kinds of work robots do. Your teacher or librarian can make suggestions about sources of information. When you have finished your research, you'll write a report about "working robots." The list below has suggestions for the kind of information you should put in your report. You also can include other information you find interesting. You will need to answer some questions through your research. You can answer others by giving your own opinion.

1. Explain the work the robot does.

2. Is this work something a human worker used to do or could do?

3. Why do companies want robots to do this work instead of humans?

4. Is it better that humans no longer have to do this work?

5. Robots have caused people to lose jobs. However, has the invention of "worker robots" created new jobs for humans? What are some of those jobs?

Extra Activity

Businesses in your community might already be using robots as workers. Call the Chamber of Commerce in your town or city. It can probably give you information about any local businesses that use robots. You could visit the business or interview someone there to get your report information. Maybe your class could even take a field trip to see robots at work!

What Would Happen If...

Here is another way to understand how people in society depend on other people to do their jobs. Think about what would happen if people *didn't* do their jobs. Follow the instructions below to find out.

Directions

In the left-hand column below, list all the different kinds of jobs people work at in your school. In the right-hand column, write what would happen if those workers did not do their jobs.

Workers in My School	What Would Happen If...

Activity Sheet #76
Individual or small-group activity

On Strike!

Sometimes workers in our society go on *strike*. This means that they stop doing their work because they are unhappy with their working conditions. Some workers have jobs that are so important to society that it's against the law for them to go on strike. Follow the instructions below to discover what kinds of jobs are vital to our society.

Directions

In the left-hand column below, list workers who you think shouldn't go on strike (because the strike would have a very serious effect on everyone). In the middle column, write what would happen if those workers did strike. Also, check the right column if you think it's against the law for these workers to strike.

Workers in Society	What Would Happen If These Workers Went on Strike?	Against the Law?

What Are Goods and Services?

Some people have jobs where they make things like cars, a loaf of bread, a pair of shoes, or a TV. These things are called *goods*. Other people have jobs where they don't make things. They help people by doing something for them—for example, repairing a car, cleaning clothes, cutting someone's hair, or selling a pair of shoes. These activities provide *services*. Follow the instructions below to learn more about goods and services.

Directions

You can do this activity by yourself or in a small group. You will need a telephone book for research purposes.

1. Look at the part of the telephone book where businesses advertise. This is usually the yellow pages.

2. Use two pieces of your own paper. Write "Goods" at the top of one sheet of paper and "Services" at the top of the other sheet.

3. Read the yellow pages of the phone book. Make one list of the goods produced by businesses. Make another list of the services offered. If you do this in small groups, divide the yellow pages between the groups. Have one group do sections A through H, one group do I through P, and the last group Q through Z, for example.

4. Compare your lists with other groups' lists. Did you all agree on what types of things were goods and what were services? Discuss any differences.

Extra Activity

Want Ad Research

Instead of using the phone book, use the want ad section of the newspaper.

Services for Your Home

Your home is a place that needs a lot of servicing. For example, some things might break and need to be fixed. Other services, such as carpet cleaning, may be required. Follow the instructions below to discover all the service jobs needed to keep a home running.

Directions

People hire a lot of other people to perform services for their homes. In the left-hand column, list all the service work you can think of that a house might need. If you can think of a job title for the person who would do that work, write it in the right-hand column. An example is done for you.

Service Needed For A House	Job Title
The shower is leaking.	Plumber

Where Do Goods Come From?

People in our society depend on workers all across the United States. Many goods that you buy are made in different states. Sometimes the raw materials needed to make a good come from one state, but the product is made in another. Every state has certain goods or raw materials that they produce. Do the following activity to discover what they are.

Directions

Select one or more states. If you work in groups, you might want to take a few. Your teacher can help you decide which states to choose. Use your social studies book and/or an encyclopedia to research your state(s).

1. Research your state(s) to discover what products or raw materials it produces.

2. Get a large piece of paper. Draw a map of your state. Write the goods and raw materials that your state produces on your map. You might draw illustrations on the map, too.

3. Share the results of your research with your class. You may make a bulletin board with all the maps.

Activity Sheet #80
Individual or class activity

The Global Economy

Our world and the work we do are changing. We now live in a time when goods are produced in a *global economy*. What does that mean? It means that goods and raw materials come from countries all over the world. This activity will help you learn more about the global economy. It might also improve your geography skills!

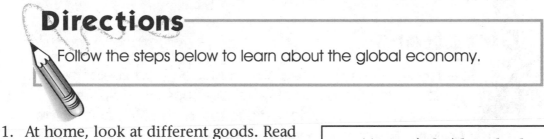

Directions

Follow the steps below to learn about the global economy.

1. At home, look at different goods. Read their tags and labels to find out where they came from. You can look at clothes, appliances, furniture, or anything that tells where it was made.

Materials Needed

- Straight pins
- Small pieces of paper
- World map on a bulletin board
- Tape

2. Make a list of 10 items and where they were made. Try to find items that were made in different places. You do not have to find 10 different items. You may have, for example, several articles of clothing. But try to use as many different things as you can. Bring your list to school.

3. Using straight pins, paper, and tape, make small flags. Write the name of a product and the place it came from on each flag, for example, "Shoes/South Korea." Each student should make 10 flags.

4. Take turns putting your flags on the world map. Put each product flag on the country where the product was made.

5. Have someone read the names of all the products made in different countries. Discuss what you discover. What have you learned about the global economy?

Goods from Around the World

People in our country now depend on workers all across the world. Many of the goods that you buy are made in different countries. Sometimes the raw materials needed to make a good come from one country and the product is made in another country. Different countries produce certain goods or raw materials. Do the following activity to discover what they are.

Directions

Select one country to research. Your teacher can help you decide which country to choose. Use your social studies book and/or an encyclopedia to research your country. This activity also can be done in a small group.

1. Research your country. Discover what products or raw materials it is known for producing. Find out if people in the United States buy goods that are made there. What countries does your country sell its goods to?

2. Get a large piece of paper. Draw a map of your country. Write the goods and raw materials it produces on your map. You might want to draw illustrations on the map, too.

3. Write a short report to attach to your map. Describe the countries that your country sells goods to.

4. Display your map in the classroom.